Monologues and Dialogues about

ORDINARY PEOPLE-
Extraordinary
GOD

Vol. 2

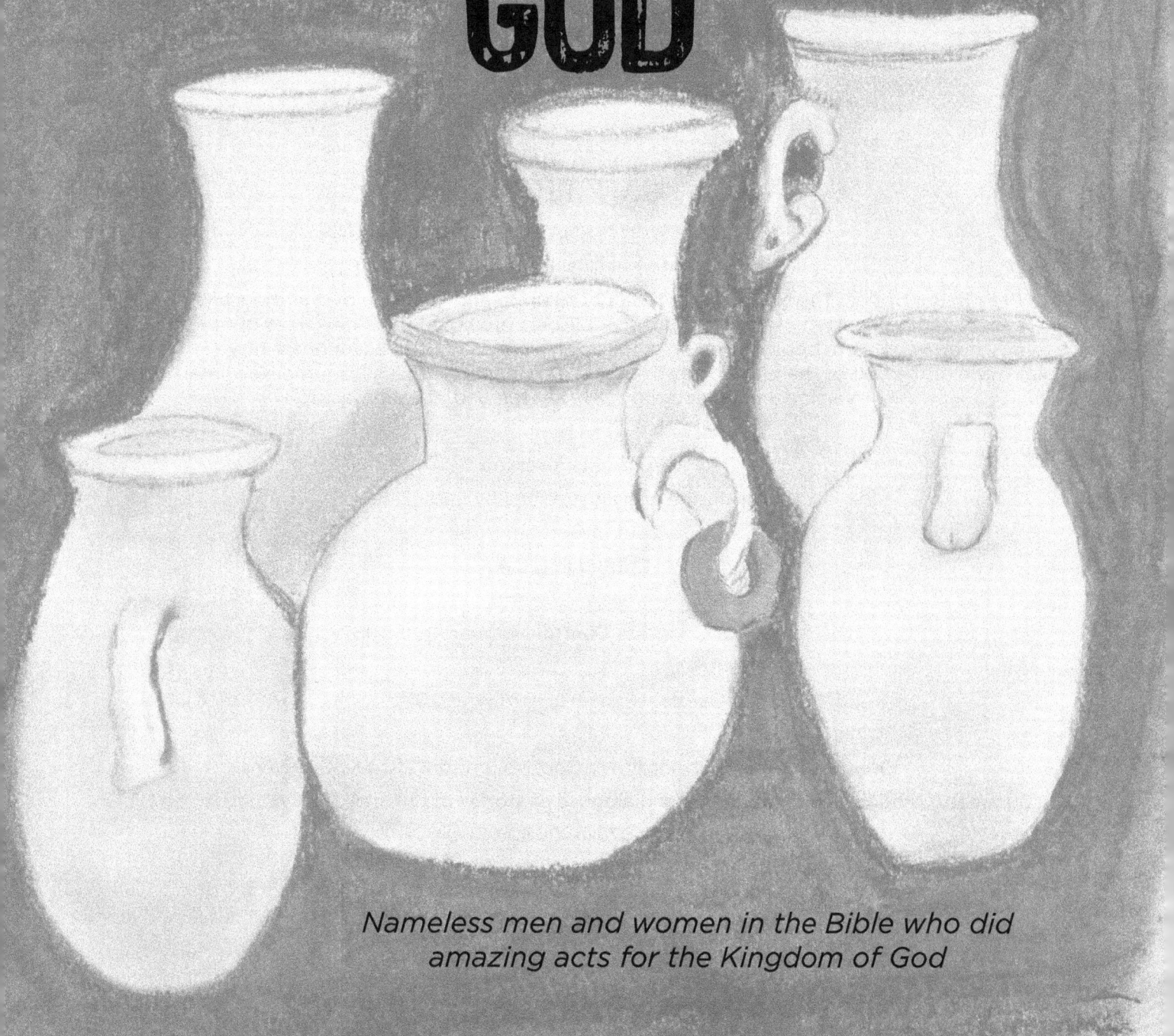

Nameless men and women in the Bible who did amazing acts for the Kingdom of God

Michael E. Owens
Illustrations by Leda Owens

Illustrations by Leda Owens

Ordinary People – Extraordinary God
Volume 2

Published by

Scribblers Press

9741 SE 174th Place Road, Summerfield, Florida 34491

Printed by

Trinity Press

3190 Reps Miller Road, Suite 360, Norcross, Georgia 30071

Library of Congress Control Number: 2019911827

Owens, Michael E., 07/04/2020

Ordinary People- Extraordinary God, Volume 2 / Michael E. Owens

Summary: A book of monologues and dialogues of stories of unnamed individuals in the Bible

ISBN: 978-1-950308-17-0

Table of Contents

Introduction

This is Volume 2 of monologues of various Bible characters – men and women – who have remained nameless through the centuries. These discourses are designed to be performed in Bible costumes in front of congregations of believers and non-believers. Before I thought of writing a book about these characters, I often though about these people and wondered about who they were, what brought them to this moment in their lives and how this encounter with God changed their very being. I wished to know about their lives, their livelihood, their families, their views, how they felt as well as what happened to them after their encounter with God. These stories are not found in the Bible, but rather they are assumptions of what might have occurred with each of these special people. I rather see these stories as what I call "Sanctified Imaginations". I have tried to give a voice and a life to each of the individuals. Of course, there can be, and there are, many opinions and views about these personalities. I don't argue the point. Your ideas may be very different from mine, and that's fine. Use this book to spur your own imagination if you want; or use what is within these pages to tell the wonderful stories of these unique and exceptional, unnamed people of God.

When I tell these stories, I always do it with an appropriate costume that matches the character I am portraying. In each section of the book, you will find different costuming ideas. For the most part, these were very average people and their clothes reflected their status in the community – very plain and unassuming. I have included a few commercial patterns that can be purchased to help in the construction of the various costumes.

I do not use a script while I am performing. I review the story often and tell it from the heart. There may be opportunity to add or even delete parts of the play. Use your own prayerful edition of these characters you will be portraying. Each story points to the saving grace of Jesus Christ. Make that the emphasis of each story you tell - that, through the Holy Spirit, every event and character you speak of will glorify God and His Son. Every play you perform is designed to lead people to personal salvation or to lead then into a deeper relationship with Christ. Plan that in each performance.

I would challenge you to study the Bible and find other nameless characters who have done amazing actions for the Kingdom and perform their story as well. Volume 2 contains several women parts, and Volume 3 will have more of a mix of male and female presentations.

Watch for the podcast of all the characters in the "Ordinary People – Extraordinary God" series with "The Mike and Friends Too Show" coming soon. My wife and I will present each dialogue and monologue for the podcast and you can listen how we interpret each one. Hopefully this will help you in your presentations.

I pray that as you use this book, you will be blessed to see the fruit of your ministering through drama.

Acknowledgements

Many pastors and friends have been influential in the writing of this book. Their sermons as well as their informal discussions with me, have given me a deeper insight into the characters included in this book. I have appreciated their patience and interest in my project. They have shared their sermon notes, their time and their blessing to advance my work. For this, I am eternally grateful.

Specifically, I want to thank a few of them for their help. First and foremost, I want to thank my dearest friend, Danny Hawthorne, the current pastor of Green Acres Church in Bastrop, Louisiana. Danny and I have been friends since undergraduate days at Louisiana College in Pineville, Louisiana, where we both received our bachelor's degrees. Danny had already committed to the ministry and was pursuing his life work of being a pastor. I was very honored to be with Danny as he celebrated his 50th year in the ministry in 2018. Over the years we were fortunate to be able to work together in several churches and other ministries. He was either the Youth Director or Pastor and I worked alongside him as the Music Minister. For several years we worked together at the Louisiana Correctional Institute for Women located in St. Gabriel, Louisiana under the direction of the ministry's founder, Mrs. Thelma Hebert and her daughter Karen. Danny has always been an inspiration to me through the years for his love of the Lord's work and his dedication to His church and His people. Danny and his wife, Meda as well as his children, Juliann, Jarrod, Jill, and Jayme have been a blessing and an encouragement to me throughout my life.

Additionally, my wife and I have been blessed by the calling of a new pastor, James Martin, to our church, Parkview, in Lilburn Georgia in 2019. He and his wife Lizzy and their two boys, J.J and Hudson, are definitely a Godsend to our church. His enthusiastic manner, his contagious smile and his devoted adherence to the Word of God has been a refreshing addition to our community of believers. I have gleaned much from his sermons as he has enlightened us through a study in the book of Acts in his first months as pastor. He has revealed a deep awareness and understanding of scripture that has opened our hearts and eyes to the wonders of the Holy Spirit and the workings of the early church. Several of the characters I have introduced in this book have come from his sermons. I am grateful for his willingness to share his sermon notes with me and allow me to use his voice in telling these stories.

Lastly, I want to thank my wife, Leda, for her encouragement and inspiration. She faithfully attends an early morning Bible study at the First Baptist Church in Lilburn, Georgia. I have seen her grow and mature spiritually from her involvement in this class. She regularly comes home and shares with me what she has learned from the study headed by the leader of the group, Jill Perry. These little snippets have become huge nuggets of truth and motivation that have inspired me to continue my writing.

Dedication

To our children,

Kristen Rebecca, Kyle Robertson, and Kelly Renee
M.E.O.

John Gabriel and Lydia Faye
L.N.O.

You are a gift from God to us.

CENTURION AT THE CROSS

Centurion at the Cross Costume

This costume is rather elaborate. It can be simplified to be similar with the costume for the "Jesus Heals Centurion's Servant" outfit. Sword, shield nor the helmet are essential, but add to the character. The tunic with belt, sandals would be sufficient.

Centurion at the Cross – Matthew 27:45-54

The Scripture:

From noon until three in the afternoon darkness came over all the land. 46 About three in the afternoon Jesus cried out in a loud voice, "Eli, Eli, lema sabachthani?" (which means "My God, my God, why have you forsaken me?").

47 When some of those standing there heard this, they said, "He's calling Elijah."

48 Immediately one of them ran and got a sponge. He filled it with wine vinegar, put it on a staff, and offered it to Jesus to drink. 49 The rest said, "Now leave him alone. Let's see if Elijah comes to save him."

50 And when Jesus had cried out again in a loud voice, he gave up his spirit.

51 At that moment the curtain of the temple was torn in two from top to bottom. The earth shook, the rocks split 52 and the tombs broke open. The bodies of many holy people who had died were raised to life. 53 They came out of the tombs after Jesus' resurrection and went into the holy city and appeared to many people.

54 When the centurion and those with him who were guarding Jesus saw the earthquake and all that had happened, they were terrified, and exclaimed, "Surely he was the Son of God!"

The Preparation:

COSTUME – The costume for this character should be similar to a Centurion soldier. A helmet, sword and shield would be appropriate but not necessary.

AGE – This character can be at any age, as an adult.

BACKGROUND – This is a Roman soldier who was used to taking orders in a matter-of-fact manner.

DEMEANOR – He was in charge and would appear to be authoritarian.

The Story:

It was the strangest day I have ever seen in my lifetime. Ever. It didn't start out strange. It started out as a normal day; well, as normal as a day could be for a crucifixion. Crucifixions were nothing new or strange. With the Roman government, a crucifixion was a regular occurrence. Having a crucifixion was not the strange thing, at least at first. I guess it was more of WHO we are crucifying than anything.

I don't want to get ahead of my story. So, let me give you some background. I am a Roman soldier. Without saying, Roman soldiers are the best in the world. We are strong, well-trained, ready to protect Rome and the Roman citizens anywhere in the world; and above all, and I mean, above all, we are obedient to our commanders. When we are told to go, we go. When told to fight, we fight. A Roman soldier, first and foremost.

On this particular day I had been assigned to duty in the city of Jerusalem. Take my word for it, it's not the most favorite place to be appointed. The Jews and their authorities were not the greatest group to supervise. Sometimes their demands could be downright petty to say the least. But to keep peace, the Roman government gave them a lot of latitude to deal with their issues. As long it didn't interfere with us, we didn't interfere with them.

But these last few days, the last week in fact, you might say it wasn't typical at all. Of course, this particular problem involved the religious zealots from the temple. Then again, almost all our disputes with the Jews involved their religious zealots.

It all involved the arrival to Jerusalem of a man called Jesus. What an entrance He made. It was a genuine spectacle. He entered the city on a donkey - just like a conquering King. And the people were going wild – laying palm leaves and their cloaks in his path and giving him praises. What a lot of hoopla! Even the Romans liked a good parade!

Then he did the most amazing thing. He rode up to the temple and started to throw out the money changers and anyone else who was buying and selling there. Ha! Even the Roman army enjoys a good fight!

But then, before the week was out, it seemed there was this unbelievable turn around. It appeared those Jewish religious nuts had transformed the people into to a frenzy against Jesus. What a strange turn of events.

I don't know what all happened the rest of the week. There was an incident in a garden, I know that. It seemed they gave this Jesus a trial, it you want to call it that; and he was convicted of claiming to be the Son of God. What? Now, the Roman army was drawn into this. How did that happen? And then, behold, he was to be crucified! Amazing! He came into Jerusalem as a king and now he is a criminal.

Now, on top of that, I have been drawn into the fray. I was on crucifixion duty. Most of the time these assignments never bothered me, but this one was different. Here he was – a simple man. He seemed to have no riches, nor did he have any prominent position in government. Yet, he was called "The King of the Jews". He came, riding into the city, now he leaves it carrying his own cross; not hailed as a King, but now spat upon and beaten as a prisoner. Go figure.

He was placed on the cross and nails were driven through his hands and feet. I watched as the cross was thrust into the ground. I heard him speak to another who was being crucified at the same time – telling him about paradise.

The chief priests were there along with lawyers and elders, mocking him.

But then everything around us changed. About noon, it got very dark – a very strange eeriness covered the landscape. Then Jesus cried out, "My God, my God, why have you forsaken me?"

As I watched, I saw him breathe his last and suddenly an earthquake shook the hillside and rocks, tossing everyone to the ground. Get this - Graves opened, the dead walked about, and we were petrified with fear.

At this point, I knew the truth. This was no ordinary man, no ordinary criminal. No, this had to be the Son of God.

My life changed after what I witnessed that day. I knew that Jesus was more than a carpenter, more than a religious oddity, more than merely a leader of a band of crazed disciples.

I knew I needed to seek out his followers, find out about this Jesus, this Son of God, this King of the Jews. And I did. Now, I am a follower of the Christ. I have a Savior who had forgiven me of my sins and offered me eternal life in Him. Although I was there when He was crucified and I watched Him die, He did not stay dead for long. Three days He was in that tomb, and then He came out alive; and He lives today. He lives in my heart. He can live in your heart too. Ask Him to come in, forgive your sins and He will offer you a joyous life eternal. Do it today.

FOUR MEN AND A FUNERAL (OR TWO)

Four Men and a Funeral (or Two) Costume

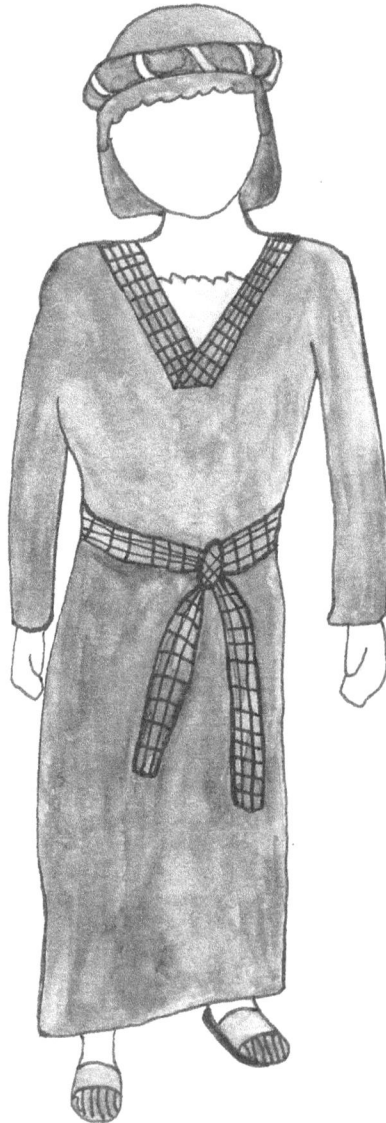

This costume is rather simple. Any color would do, just not too fancy. Some headpiece would be appropriate. The tunic with belt, sandals would be sufficient.

Four Men and a Funeral (or Two) Acts 4:32 to 5:14

(From a Sermon presented by Pastor James Martin, Parkview Church, Lilburn, Georgia titled "What about Hypocrisy in the Church?" 2020)

The Scriptures:

[32] All the believers were one in heart and mind. No one claimed that any of their possessions was their own, but they shared everything they had. [33] With great power the apostles continued to testify to the resurrection of the Lord Jesus. And God's grace was so powerfully at work in them all [34] that there were no needy persons among them. For from time to time those who owned land or houses sold them, brought the money from the sales [35] and put it at the apostles' feet, and it was distributed to anyone who had need.

[36] Joseph, a Levite from Cyprus, whom the apostles called Barnabas (which means "son of encouragement"), [37] sold a field he owned and brought the money and put it at the apostles' feet.

[1] Now a man named Ananias, together with his wife Sapphira, also sold a piece of property. [2] With his wife's full knowledge he kept back part of the money for himself but brought the rest and put it at the apostles' feet.

[3] Then Peter said, "Ananias, how is it that Satan has so filled your heart that you have lied to the Holy Spirit and have kept for yourself some of the money you received for the land? [4] Didn't it belong to you before it was sold? And after it was sold, wasn't the money at your disposal? What made you think of doing such a thing? You have not lied just to human beings but to God."

[5] When Ananias heard this, he fell down and died. And great fear seized all who heard what had happened. [6] Then some young men came forward, wrapped up his body, and carried him out and buried him.

[7] About three hours later his wife came in, not knowing what had happened. [8] Peter asked her, "Tell me, is this the price you and Ananias got for the land?"

"Yes," she said, "that is the price."

[9] Peter said to her, "How could you conspire to test the Spirit of the Lord? Listen! The feet of the men who buried your husband are at the door, and they will carry you out also."

[10] At that moment she fell down at his feet and died. Then the young men came in and, finding her dead, carried her out and buried her beside her husband. [11] Great fear seized the whole church and all who heard about these events.

The Preparation:

COSTUME – The costume for this character should be a simple Bible outfit.

AGE – This character can be at any age but is written for a younger person to perform. Can be an older person, just note that in the story.

BACKGROUND – This is a new Christian

DEMEANOR – He is overwhelmed and a little surprised, but then realizes what is happening.

The Story:

Been to a funeral lately? Been a pallbearer at one? How about two funerals – in the same day and being a pallbearer at both? Let me tell you my story.

I was a young man then – a new follower of Jesus Christ. I had heard the preaching of Peter and God got a hold of my heart and I became a Christian. Being new to the faith, I was anxious to know more. I was there when Peter walked past the Beautiful Gate and healed the lame man. I had passed that place many, many times and saw him there, waiting for alms. This healing convinced me to follow Jesus and that event gave Peter another opportunity to preach Jesus to the people.

I watched as they were confronted by the Sanhedrin along with the priests and the captain of the temple guard. These men, Peter and John, showed no weakness and had no fear in front of these religious leaders. The elite considered them to be unlearned men. Neither had any rabbinic training, yet they spoke with such authority and boldness! And because of their preaching, they were arrested and put in jail. It seemed that the more the church was persecuted, the more it grew.

What a wonderful community of believers! They were all supportive and helpful to each other. We seemed to be all of one heart. If there was one in need of anything, someone would step up and provide whatever was needed.

There was one man in particular I remember by the name of Joseph, or as the apostles called him, Barnabas. He had a field that he sold, and he brought the money to the apostles and laid it at their feet. What an act of grace and kindness. Everyone of us praised God for his generosity. Now, not everyone had a means of sharing like Barnabas did. But there were others who did share also. This is where my story begins.

We were gathered together to hear Peter and John tell us what had happened with their meeting with the religious leaders and their time in jail. We had been praying, and the Holy Spirit had filled our hearts to the point that the place where we were meeting seemed to shake. After Barnabas had made his offering, a man named Ananias made his offering to the apostles as well. He too had sold land and he told the church leaders he as giving it all to those in need. Wow! What another amazing contribution. We were about to praise God and thank Ananias for the gift; but Peter threw a wet blanket on the celebration. Peter spoke brazenly to Ananias and said, "Ananias, how is it that Satan has filled your heart?"

What? We were all in shock! Satan had filled his heart? How is that so? Was he not giving a gift to God to help those in need?

Peter continued, "You have lied to the Holy Spirit and have kept for yourself some of the money you received for the land. Didn't it belong to you before it was sold? And after it was sold, wasn't the money at your disposal? What made you think of doing such a thing? You have not lied just to human beings but to God."

What a revelation! The entire place was stunned; but before we could say a word, Ananias dropped dead; right at that moment Talk about a shocker! Believe me when I say, great fear gripped every heart in the place.

I was just standing there in amazement, along with several of my other friends. Then, Peter motioned to us and we knew what he wanted us to do. We wrapped the body, took him out and buried him straightaway.

About three hours later, we had just finished the burial and returned to the gathering. At the same time, Ananias' wife, Sapphira entered the place. She had not heard about her husband.

Peter asked her, "Tell me, is this the price you and Ananias got for the land?"

"Yes," she said, "that is the price."

Peter said to her, "How could you conspire to test the Spirit of the Lord? Listen! The feet of the men who buried your husband are at the door, and they will carry you out also."

At that moment she fell down at his feet and died.

Of course, we had just entered when we heard Peter's words. We thought she had just fainted when hearing her husband's death. But when we went to her, she was dead too! We carried her out and buried her beside her husband.

You think people were scared before? Now there was great fear that seized the whole church and all who heard about these events.

So, what does all this mean? It surely made the people uncomfortable – back then and still today.

Some see the wrath of God and think 'how unfair! God is too harsh.'

Others say, 'It's Peter's fault, he placed a curse on them, it was too much pressure and they died from heart attacks.'

Both views are mistaken. You would think giving to the church would be a good thing, but that is not the point either. Not everyone had land to sell and then give the proceeds to the church. Those that could, did; those that didn't, couldn't.

The point is, Ananias and Sapphira lied to God – not to man, but to the Holy Spirit. This was a body of believers called the church and God calls all Christians to remain holy and pure.

Ananias and Sapphira showed deceit and hypocrisy to the church. It's not that they didn't give enough, or that they kept some of the money for themselves. It is about the fact that they lied and then pretended they were giving it all. They had seen the favor given to Barnabas and they wanted to claim favor for themselves. They wanted others to see their supposed generosity and they wanted to bask in their claim of giving it all to God.

But their lie was exposed and when it was revealed, they died.

This teaches us the role of human consciousness, honesty and integrity. Ananias and Sapphira failed to keep their conscious clean, they failed to hate sin and they failed to maintain truth. Their sin found them out.

What do I say to you? Walk in the light. Maintain a clear conscious. Live transparent before your brothers and sisters in Christ. Come clean before God.

John once wrote, "If we confess our sin, He is faithful and just to forgive us our sin and to cleanse us from all unrighteousness."

THE FORTUNE-TELLING SLAVE GIRL

The Fortune-Telling Slave Girl Costume

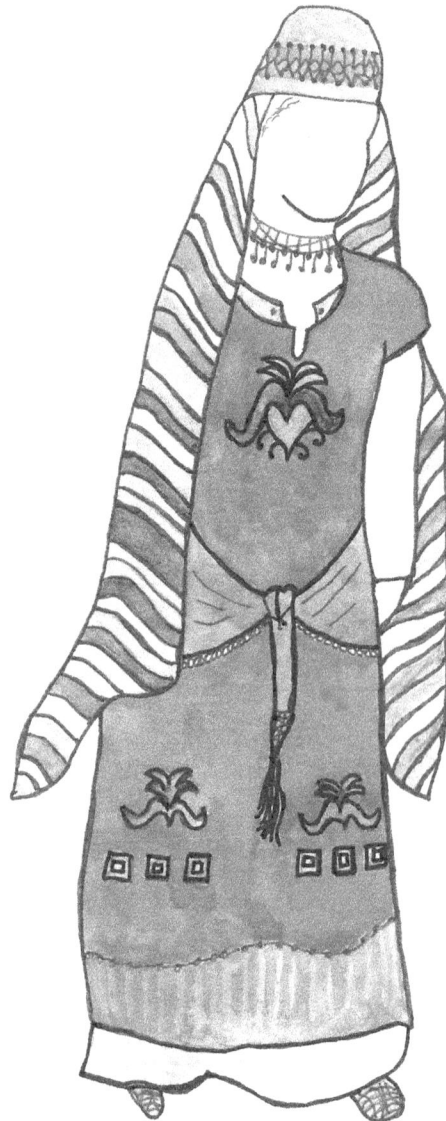

This costume is rather elaborate. Se was dressed to attract attention and draw passersby to her. Adding tassels or other bling to the outfit would dress it up somewhat. Use your own creativity to enhance the costume.

The Fortune-Telling Slave Girl – Acts 16:16-24

The Scripture:

16 Once when we were going to the place of prayer, we were met by a female slave who had a spirit by which she predicted the future. She earned a great deal of money for her owners by fortune-telling. 17 She followed Paul and the rest of us, shouting, "These men are servants of the Most High God, who are telling you the way to be saved." 18 She kept this up for many days. Finally, Paul became so annoyed that he turned around and said to the spirit, "In the name of Jesus Christ I command you to come out of her!" At that moment the spirit left her.

19 When her owners realized that their hope of making money was gone, they seized Paul and Silas and dragged them into the marketplace to face the authorities. 20 They brought them before the magistrates and said, "These men are Jews, and are throwing our city into an uproar 21 by advocating customs unlawful for us Romans to accept or practice."

22 The crowd joined in the attack against Paul and Silas, and the magistrates ordered them to be stripped and beaten with rods. 23 After they had been severely flogged, they were thrown into prison, and the jailer was commanded to guard them carefully. 24 When he received these orders, he put them in the inner cell and fastened their feet in the stocks.

The Preparation:

COSTUME – The costume for this character could be one, she could be well dressed in bangles and other jewelry, or she could be poor with very simple unadorned clothes.

AGE – This character can be at any age, but possibly younger

BACKGROUND – This was a young woman who was a slave and did as she was told to do.

DEMEANOR – Mysterious at first, but then relieved that she was freed for the demons.

The Story:

I knew things. Lots of things. Things I would repeat and things I never wanted to repeat. Oh, but I made money – lots of money. Of course, not for me, but for those who owned me. Want to know your future? I could tell you. In a moment I would know all about you. Sometimes you would want to hear what I said. Other times it would leave you in tears, or worse, in hysterics. It made no never-mind to me. I plied my trade all along the coast in Macedonia, but especially in Philippi. I had been like this most of my life, at least as long as I could remember. When others found out I possessed this special talent, I became important property to anyone who owned me. Throughout my life I was bought and sold many times. This is where my story begins.

At first I assumed the meeting with Paul and Silas was purely coincidental. I just happened to meet them as they were heading to a place of prayer. But right away I knew who they were. Their spirits spoke loudly to me. For the first time in my life I seemed to have little control over what I was saying. And I had little control over my body. It seemed to be pulled in the direction of these men. I followed them for days. I don't know how they put up with me, shouting at them for all the world to hear.

"These men are servants of the Most High God, who are telling you the way to be saved. These men are servants of the Most High God, who are telling you the way to be saved."

I'm not sure why they did not stop me earlier, but this went on for days. I became such an annoyance to Paul and the others, he finally stopped, turned around and shouted at me,

"In the name of Jesus Christ, I command you to come out of her!" At that moment the spirit left her.

I don't know what happened next. I do know I fell to the ground, and it seemed a great heaviness was pulled from my body. My masters, who have been following me, rushed to pick me up. Immediately they realized the spirit to tell fortunes had left me, as well as their means of making money.

In fact, they were so enraged, that grabbed Paul and Silas and dragged them both before the magistrates in the marketplace. I heard them claim,

"These men are Jews and are throwing our city into an uproar by advocating customs unlawful for us Romans to accept or practice."

The crowd also joined in the attack against Paul and Silas, and the authorities ordered them to be stripped and beaten with rods. After they had been severely flogged, they were thrown into prison, and the jailer was commanded to guard them carefully.

I had witnessed it all. Later, I heard that when the jailer received the orders, he put them in the inner cell and fastened their feet in the stocks.

Of course, there was no concern for me. To those who owned me, I mattered nothing. I thought to myself, What is to become of me? Where do I go?

At that moment, a woman I had seen often in the Philippi marketplace, a seller of purple, came to me and lifted me up. She looked softly into my eyes and said,

"Praise God you no longer have to pander to those men. Christ has set you free. Come with me. There is a place for you. Paul and Silas were recent guests in my home."

She told me her name was Lydia, and she had become a follower of Jesus. She said Paul and Silas had come to the river outside the city gate where she and many other women had gathered. There they heard the preaching about Jesus.

"The Lord opened my heart," she said to me, "And as they spoke, I knew I must give my life to Jesus and be saved."

"This is what my demons called out to them," I said. And then I asked Lydia to show me the way to be saved.

I have a new life now. I am no longer condemned by the evil spirit that inhabited me.

There may be some of you who have given in to spirits which want to destroy you and keep you from your true calling and to keep you from the peace in your heart that only Christ can give. Satan has sent his demons to destroy us and our testimony and to keep us from giving our all to Jesus. Let Christ set yourself free.

.

THE HEALING
AT THE POOL

The Healing at the Pool Costume

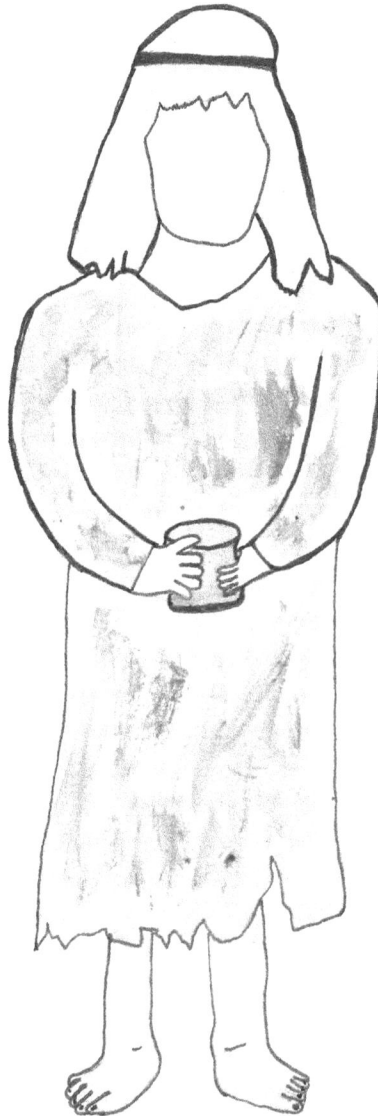

This costume is very simple. Any muted, earthy color would do. Some headpiece would be appropriate. Barefoot would be good. Outfit could be discolored and ragged.

The Healing at the Pool – John 5:2-15

The Scripture:

Some time later, Jesus went up to Jerusalem for one of the Jewish festivals. ² Now there is in Jerusalem near the Sheep Gate a pool, which in Aramaic is called Bethesda and which is surrounded by five covered colonnades. ³ Here a great number of disabled people used to lie—the blind, the lame, the paralyzed.⁴ᵇ ⁵ One who was there had been an invalid for thirty-eight years. ⁶ When Jesus saw him lying there and learned that he had been in this condition for a long time, he asked him, "Do you want to get well?"

⁷ "Sir," the invalid replied, "I have no one to help me into the pool when the water is stirred. While I am trying to get in, someone else goes down ahead of me."

⁸ Then Jesus said to him, "Get up! Pick up your mat and walk." ⁹ At once the man was cured; he picked up his mat and walked.

The day on which this took place was a Sabbath, ¹⁰ and so the Jewish leaders said to the man who had been healed, "It is the Sabbath; the law forbids you to carry your mat."

¹¹ But he replied, "The man who made me well said to me, 'Pick up your mat and walk.' "

¹² So they asked him, "Who is this fellow who told you to pick it up and walk?"

¹³ The man who was healed had no idea who it was, for Jesus had slipped away into the crowd that was there.

¹⁴ Later Jesus found him at the temple and said to him, "See, you are well again. Stop sinning or something worse may happen to you." ¹⁵ The man went away and told the Jewish leaders that it was Jesus who had made him well.

The Preparation:

COSTUME – The costume for this character would be standard Bible clothing. Maybe a little worn and/or tattered

AGE – At least 38 years or older.

BACKGROUND – Angry with the Religious group. Grateful to God for the healing

DEMEANOR – Totally enthusiastic!

The Story:

Sabbath or not, this guy is blessed! I was healed, and I could care less if it was the Sabbath or some other day of the week. Do you know how many years I have been waiting there, by that pool, and I never, never touched the water? Thirty-eight years! Did you hear me? Thirty-eight long, agonizing, frustrating, excruciating years I laid there! People passing that pool every day, passing me every day, over and over again they passed me. Never looking my way, never helping me into the pool! Do you think I cared it was the Sabbath! Not on your life!

Those religious high-minded, ridged, mean spirited, unhelpful group of stuffed robes, had the nerve to tell me the law forbids me to carry my mat! Surely they knew who I was. They saw me many, many times and ignored me just as many. There I laid by the pool, crippled and now they see me walking and all they can say is "the law forbids you to carry your mat"? Unbelievable!

Sorry, sorry, sorry but that whole scene made me so mad. The more I thought about it, the angrier I became. But I am way ahead of my story. There is a good part and that's what I want to share with you now.

Okay, I'm calm now.

Yes, I had been there sitting by the pool of Bethesda for almost thirty-eight years. I had been an invalid for the thirty-eight years and almost all of it spend, waiting by that pool for my turn to get into the waters whenever the springs that fed the pool would cause the waters to be stirred. There were many, many others who were there with me – waiting. Some were blind, others who where lame like me, there were other infirmities and sicknesses I did not know or understand. Were they healed by getting in the pool? Some said yes, they were, and I believed them. Others also claimed to be healed, but I had my doubts. Of course, I never had the opportunity to try the pool. Every time I tried to get in, someone else got in first. Would the waters have healed me? I would never know. But then again, I would not have to know.

Jesus, whom I had never met nor would have known, had come to Jerusalem during the time of one of the festivals. He was passing by the pool when He noticed me lying there. While He stood there, looking at me, someone said I had been in this condition for a long time. Then this man, whom I did not know, said to me, "Do you want to get well?"

I thought, *What a silly question. Thirty-eight years I have tried to "get well" but never could. Of course, I wanted to get well. Is this man going to help into the pool or not?* But, I was polite and civil.

"Sir," I replied, "I have no one to help me into the pool when the water is stirred. While I am trying to get in, someone else goes down ahead of me."

Then the man said to me, "Get up! Pick up your mat and walk." What did I just hear? Do you not think if I could have just "gotten up", I would have? But behold, as I tried to get up, new strength at once seemed to come to my legs, and I was able to stand. Not only was I able to stand, but I could walk, wait, I could jump, hop, run! I was astonished! Shocked that I was cured; I picked up my mat and walked- no I ran and leaped though the temple.

I did not think it important, but the day on which this took place was a Sabbath, and would the Jewish leaders notice I was healed and congratulate me? Did they praise God for what happened to me? Did they rejoice over my good fortune? No! They did not! Do you know what they had the audacity to say to me? They looked at me, a healed man, the result of a miracle after thirty-eight years. They said to the me, "It is the Sabbath; the law forbids you to carry your mat."

What? Of course, I was carrying my mat! I was told to get up, pick up my mat and WALK!

Then I answered them, "The man who made me well said to me, 'Pick up your mat and walk.' " Wasn't the healing more important than the mat?

So, then they asked me, "Who is this fellow who told you to pick it up and walk?"

I realized at that point; I had no idea who had healed me. I had glanced around but the man had slipped away into the crowd that was there.

Later that day he found me in the temple, and he said to me, "See, you are well again. Stop sinning or something worse may happen to you."

This time I asked him, "Who are you?" And the man told me His name was Jesus. After he went away, I told the Jewish leaders that it was Jesus who had made me well.

You think they were happy? No way! You would think they would be pleased, but no, they just started talking about ways they wanted to kill Him. Can you believe that?

Now, this story is not about the religious leaders. I don't mean that at all. This story is about Jesus and me.

You see, I didn't let it go. I became a follower of Jesus. Which means now, I could follow Him. Now, I could walk, thanks to Him. I was able to hear Him teach many times.

So, what am I trying to say? I am grateful to Jesus for seeing my need and answering it. I was a nobody, a poor crippled man who was of no value to anyone. But that did not stop Jesus. I didn't even know who He was, but He knew me. He was there to lift me up, to give me hope, and to forgive my sins and to lead me on a path to eternal life. Have you made that commitment to Jesus as the Savior of your life? God is keeping you safe for a reason. He is giving you an opportunity to accept Him as your Lord. Accept that opportunity to find new life in Him.

JESUS HEALS THE CENTURION'S SERVANT

Jesus Heals the Centurion's Servant Costume

This costume is of a soldier but could be very plain. The tunic with belt, sandals would be sufficient. Use anything else that might enhance the look of a soldier.

Jesus Heals the Centurion's Servant– Luke 7:1-10

The Scripture

[1] When Jesus had finished saying all this to the people who were listening, he entered Capernaum. [2] There a centurion's servant, whom his master valued highly, was sick and about to die. [3] The centurion heard of Jesus and sent some elders of the Jews to him, asking him to come and heal his servant. [4] When they came to Jesus, they pleaded earnestly with him, "This man deserves to have you do this, [5] because he loves our nation and has built our synagogue." [6] So Jesus went with them.

He was not far from the house when the centurion sent friends to say to him: "Lord, don't trouble yourself, for I do not deserve to have you come under my roof. [7] That is why I did not even consider myself worthy to come to you. But say the word, and my servant will be healed. [8] For I myself am a man under authority, with soldiers under me. I tell this one, 'Go,' and he goes; and that one, 'Come,' and he comes. I say to my servant, 'Do this,' and he does it."

[9] When Jesus heard this, he was amazed at him, and turning to the crowd following him, he said, "I tell you, I have not found such great faith even in Israel." [10] Then the men who had been sent returned to the house and found the servant well.

The Preparation:

COSTUME – The costume for this character should be as close to a soldier's costume as possible, although no need for a sword, shield or helmet.

AGE – This character can be at any age as an adult.

BACKGROUND – This had been a soldier all his life

DEMEANOR - His approach would be matt-of-fact.

The Story:

Are there any of you who have been in the army? Some of you may have served in wars, others in peace time. But one thing is clear. Wherever you served, whenever you served, you obeyed orders. I too was like that. Whatever my commander told me, I did. As a soldier under his direct authority, I was privileged to witness an amazing event. But I am a little ahead of my story.

In my specific case, I served under a kind and benevolent leader. He was God-fearing and just. Not a Roman citizen, he was a Gentile, but well respected in the

Capernaum community where he was stationed. He often gave to the poor. The religious leaders in and around the town had great respect and admiration for him. He cared not only about the men under his command, but he cared for his household staff as well, especially one certain servant.

This is where our story begins.

The servant had become ill; deathly ill. Doctors had been called. Various men of medicine had all offered their assistance and advice to help heal this servant, but all to no avail. He was going to die. I was a little surprised he had not succumbed to his illness already. But he was strong and was fighting to stay alive.

Then the commander heard the news that Jesus was preaching and healing nearby and was traveling in Capernaum. Immediately, he sent for the elders of the Jews. He believed these elders could be more persuasive than himself or a troop of soldiers traipsing to see him.

"Go find Jesus. Tell Hm of my beloved servant. Bid Jesus come and heal him," he directed them.

I guess the elders were envisioning Jesus being a hard sell. They probably thought He would be too busy, too tired or too insulted to visit the home of a Gentile. The elders probably felt they would have to plea and beg Jesus to go with them. And so they began when they approached Jesus with their petition.

"This man has a servant who is ill and very near death. This man deserves to have you do this, because he loves our nation and has built our synagogue." Before they could finish their requests, Jesus got up and went with them.

Jesus was not far from the house when the centurion sent friends to speak to him.

"Tell Jesus, 'Don't trouble yourself, for I do not deserve to have you come under my roof.'" The centurion continued, "That is why I did not even consider myself worthy to come to you."

Then the centurion spoke to Jesus and said the most amazing thing.

He said, "Say the word, and my servant will be healed. For I myself am a man under authority, with soldiers under me. I tell this one, 'Go,' and he goes; and that one, 'Come,' and he comes. I say to my servant, 'Do this,' and he does it."

When Jesus heard this, he was amazed at the centurion as well. Jesus turned to the crowd following him, he said, "I tell you; I have not found such great faith even in Israel."

At that point, the men who had been sent to find Jesus, began to return to the house. But before they could enter, others ran out the door to meet them, proclaiming the servant was now well!

What can I day? It was a miracle. The servant began to ask questions. "Did the doctors find a cure? Did someone give me medicine? How was I healed?"

The centurion answered, "It was Jesus. He spoke the word and you were immediately healed."

"But I didn't see Him. I didn't feel Him. Where is He?" the servant asked.

"He wasn't even inside our house," his master added. "Jesus just spoke, and you were made whole again."

That day changed a lot of lives. Many of us became believers. We trusted in Him that day.

JESUS RESTORES TWO DEMON-POSSESSED MEN

Jesus Restores Two Demon-Possessed Men Costume

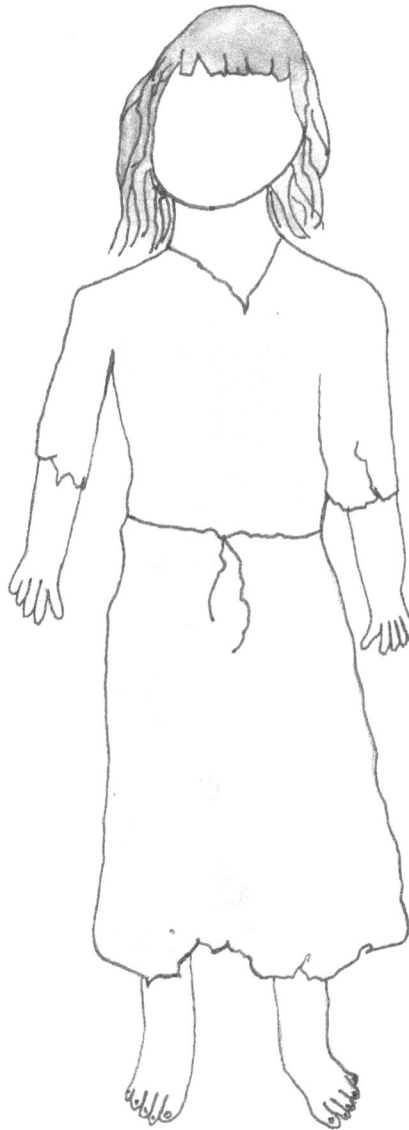

This costume is rather simple. Any muted earthy color would do.. Some headpiece would be appropriate. The tunic with belt, but no sandals would be sufficient.

Jesus Restores Two Demon-Possessed Men
Matthew 8:28-34

The Scripture:

²⁸ When he arrived at the other side in the region of the Gadarenes, two demon-possessed men coming from the tombs met him. They were so violent that no one could pass that way. ²⁹ "What do you want with us, Son of God?" they shouted. "Have you come here to torture us before the appointed time?"

³⁰ Some distance from them a large herd of pigs was feeding. ³¹ The demons begged Jesus, "If you drive us out, send us into the herd of pigs."

³² He said to them, "Go!" So, they came out and went into the pigs, and the whole herd rushed down the steep bank into the lake and died in the water. ³³ Those tending the pigs ran off, went into the town and reported all this, including what had happened to the demon-possessed men. ³⁴ Then the whole town went out to meet Jesus. And when they saw him, they pleaded with him to leave their region.

The Preparation:

COSTUME – The costume for this character should be rough and ragged. Maybe even barefoot.

AGE – This character can be at any age, but probably a little older.

BACKGROUND – This man has been demon-possessed for a long time

DEMEANOR – He is very grateful to be freed of the demons

The Story:

Is being blind worse than being deaf? Is being lame worse than being a leper? They are all terrible infirmities; infirmities that no one would want in their lives. But, I must argue being possessed by evil spirits is the worst of all. That was my plight – for a long time in my life. We talk about the "demon-possessed". But sometimes that is not true. You see, it's not normally one spirit or one demon. It's multitude of demons. There are demons of such vile and evil designs, I cannot even speak of them. But they all have names. Demons have names like greed, lust, hate, resentment, bitterness, unforgiveness, or disobedience. There are many, many more who are worse than these. Suffice to say, I was not just 'demon-possessed' but 'possessed by demons'.

I was not the only one – there were others. Others who would come and go. We lived in the tombs, south of the Sea of Galilee on the other side of the Jordan River in a land called the Gadarenes. The tombs. People thought we were banished to the tombs, sent there as punishment for our sins. Not true. The demons we possessed were drawn to the tombs. It was because we were so violent and unclean that the spirits felt at home there. No one would pass our way because we were so vicious.

That was our demons – destructive, brutal, savage, cruel and more.

But one day Jesus passed our way. This is not the normal path anyone would follow. It's on the wrong side of the Jordan and not a route to anywhere significant. The only thing we could imagine is that Jesus purposefully traveled this way to deal with us and our demons. Of course, our demons knew immediately who he was. You see, all demons recognize the Son of God, and our demons were no exception.

They would call out to Jesus.

"What do you want with us, Son of God?" they shouted. "Have you come here to torture us before the appointed time?"

The demons knew Jesus could not destroy them until after His return. There happened to be herd of pigs feeding nearby, so the demons begged Him, "If you drive us out, send us into the herd of pigs."

Jesus then said to them, "Go!" So, the demons came out of us and went into the pigs, and the whole herd rushed down the steep bank into the lake and died in the water.

Pigs. How ironic. This is almost comical. The Jewish culture thought pigs were the most unclean animal on the face of the earth. To send the demons in to pigs was no loss. No one would eat a pig. They will not be missed. But the other side of the coin were the farmers who were raising the pigs for food. Why would they be raising pigs anyway?

Well, as soon as the pigs ran off, those who were tending the pigs ran into the town and reported all this, including what had happened to the demon-possessed men. Did they stir up a hornet's nest! The whole town ran out to meet Jesus and to see what happened to the demon-possessed men.

They had neve seen anything like this before.

You would have thought they would be bringing their sick and infirmed or other possessed individuals to see Jesus, to be healed. You would have thought they would want Jesus to stay and teach them. You would have thought, right?

But when they saw him, what did they do? They pleaded with him to leave their region – to leave! I'm not kidding!

In all this hullabaloo, everyone forgot all about me. Hey, everybody; remember me, the ex- demon-possessed man? There were two of us healed that day, and neither one of us wanted to return to the tombs. The tombs had been our home for a long, long time. What do we do now? Where do we go? Will people still be afraid of us? Would anybody believe our demons had been sent from us -into a herd of pigs, no less?

Jesus had left the area and crossed back over the river to visit his own town of Capernaum. We heard he continued to do many miracles, healing the ill and infirmed.

Then as we pondered what was to come about to us, an amazing thing happened. The very same people who shunned us all those years, and the very same people who had asked Jesus to leave their region, now approached us to inquire about what Jesus did to us.

We began to explain what happened and tell them who Jesus really was. We told them how we knew who He was and about the power He had to cast out demons as the Son of God. How He had cleansed us, and through His power He was able to forgive our sins.

The townspeople were amazed, and they were sorry they asked Him to leave. Some decided to follow behind Jesus to see if He truly was the Savior. Others believed our testimony and accepted Him right then and there as the Christ we were expecting.

What does all this mean? We learned it means it doesn't matter how bad a life you lead, nor how awful you sins, nor how much you feel you are despised, nor how much you hate yourself, God loves you; just like He showed His love for us. Just like He freed us, He can free you. Trust in Him.

SABBATH AND THE WITHERED HAND

Sabbath and the Withered Hand Costume

This is a rather simple Bible costume. Any color would do, just not too fancy. Some headpiece would be appropriate. The tunic with belt, sandals would be sufficient.

Sabbath and the Withered Hand– Mark 3:1-6

The Scripture:

[1] Another time Jesus went into the synagogue, and a man with a shriveled hand was there. [2] Some of them were looking for a reason to accuse Jesus, so they watched him closely to see if he would heal him on the Sabbath. [3] Jesus said to the man with the shriveled hand, "Stand up in front of everyone."

[4] Then Jesus asked them, "Which is lawful on the Sabbath: to do good or to do evil, to save life or to kill?" But they remained silent.

[5] He looked around at them in anger and, deeply distressed at their stubborn hearts, said to the man, "Stretch out your hand." He stretched it out, and his hand was completely restored. [6] Then the Pharisees went out and began to plot with the Herodians how they might kill Jesus.

The Preparation:

COSTUME - The costume for this character should be dressed in normal Bible clothing – nothing fancy nor bright colors

AGE - This character can be at any age.

BACKGROUND – This man probably has been mocked and teased all his life.

DEMEANOR - He wants to blend in, not attract attention to himself nor his infirmity.

The Story:

I was scared. You would be too. I was a quiet man. I still am. I had gone to the synagogue to pray. That's all. In and out. That's all I wanted to do. I didn't want to make waves or cause trouble. I didn't want to be noticed. I was just about to leave when I noticed a large crowd beginning to gather behind me. As was my habit, I tended to avoid crowds. Actually, I tried to avoid people altogether. It was something I have done all my life. You see, I had a withered hand and I was ashamed of it. I had been teased and mocked and laughed as long as I could remember. I tried to hide it and the best way was to never let people see me. But today, I could not escape.

Seeing the throng of people all at once begin to crowd into the temple, I kept my head down and avoided any eye contact. I tried to move around them, but either way I moved, I was blocked. As I began to retreat, I realized these were the religious leaders of the synagogue! They were all talking angrily and loudly and I became very frightened. The only thing I could do was cower in a corner to hide myself. I was hoping they could not see me, and they would pass. But just as quickly as I knelt by the wall, the entire place became deadly quiet. *Had they noticed me?* I thought. *Was I to be punished? I had been confessing my sins, but had I missed something?* Then I heard a voice. *Was it directed at me?* I slowly turned around and everyone, and I mean everyone was looking at me! *Did I hear what I though I heard?* The voice said, "Stand up in front of everyone."

My greatest fear! I have avoided people all my life, and now I'm being asked to 'stand up in front of everyone?' You can not imagine how my heart pounded. My face flushed. Every part of me shook. I looked to see who had said that to me. But it could not have been the priest nor Pharisees. They weren't looking at me now. They were looking at the man standing over me.

As I got to my feet, this man asked the religious leaders a question. He asked them, "Which is lawful on the Sabbath: to do good or to do evil, to save life or to kill?" But they didn't say a word; just mumbling quietly to themselves. I watched as He looked around at them in anger. He seemed to be deeply distressed by their stubborn hearts. But then He slowly turned to me and said, "Stretch out your hand." At first, I recoiled and began to refuse, but His eyes seemed to beckon me. Slowly I brought my hand out from under my cloak and stretched it out. Gradually as I extended my hand, it became completely restored.

I could not believe or understand what had happened. I did not hear or see the uproar that resulted. I understand the religious leaders began to scream and yell and they stormed out of the synagogue.

I was still marveling at my hand as I wiggled my fingers and flexed then back and forth. "I am restored!" I shouted.

As I stood there I could now look around. There were many others still in the synagogue and they began to praise God and to flock around us.

Suddenly, I realized the man who told me to 'stretch out my hand' was gone. Just as quickly, many came up to me to praise God for my healing. As they clustered about, I began to ask them, "Who was the man who healed my hand?"

"Why, it was Jesus! Did you not recognize Him?" someone said to me.

"Jesus?" I asked. I had heard of Him, but I never knew who He really was.

"He really made the Pharisees mad!" another said. "Did you see how they stormed out of here? Jesus had better watch out. They seem ready to kill him for what He did!"

"Why?" I asked.

"Because Jesus healed you," someone else said.

"Me? What did I do that was so wrong?" I asked.

"He healed you on the Sabbath." was the answer.

Was it worth it to heal a man's hand and then be put to death for it? I thought.

A man who would give his life for another, would be a very special man himself. I became a follower of Jesus that day. At that point, not in the spiritual sense, but I followed Him to know more about Him. He headed for the lake and by now He had already healed many. All of those He healed seemed to be a lot worse off than me. There was those who were lame, healed; blind, healed; possessed, healed; diseased, healed; terrible infirmities, all healed by Jesus.

Of course, I still did not understand it. Why me? I only had a withered hand. Why me?

It wasn't much later as I followed Jesus around the countryside did I begin to realize the answer. I will never forget that day. A lot has happened since then. I've had a lot of time to think about what occurred. Soon, I became a follower of Jesus the Christ. I trusted Him as the Savior, sent here to save the world.

What did I learn? Jesus loves me. He cares about me. Even though I though my healing was a small thing when I viewed all those in more distress than me, He still cared. You might say I was important to Him. Think about yourself. Are there any needs in your life you think are too small for God to care? Think again. He is always there for you. Trust Him with it all.

WOMAN AND THE ALABASTER JAR

Woman and the Alabaster Jar Costume

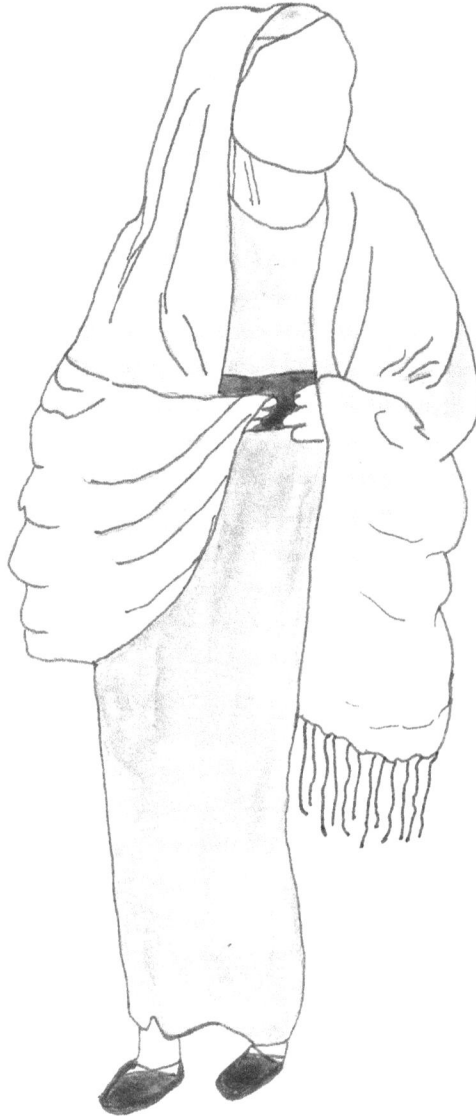

This costume is rather fancy. Bright colors; some bling. Some headpiece would be appropriate. She is a sinful woman and she attracts business with her clothing. Decorate as you see fit.

Woman and the Alabaster Jar- Luke 7:36-50

The Scripture:

36 When one of the Pharisees invited Jesus to have dinner with him, he went to the Pharisee's house and reclined at the table. 37 A woman in that town who lived a sinful life learned that Jesus was eating at the Pharisee's house, so she came there with an alabaster jar of perfume. 38 As she stood behind him at his feet weeping, she began to wet his feet with her tears. Then she wiped them with her hair, kissed them and poured perfume on them.

39 When the Pharisee who had invited him saw this, he said to himself, "If this man were a prophet, he would know who is touching him and what kind of woman she is—that she is a sinner."

40 Jesus answered him, "Simon, I have something to tell you."

"Tell me, teacher," he said.

41 "Two people owed money to a certain moneylender. One owed him five hundred denarii,[c] and the other fifty. 42 Neither of them had the money to pay him back, so he forgave the debts of both. Now which of them will love him more?"

43 Simon replied, "I suppose the one who had the bigger debt forgiven."

"You have judged correctly," Jesus said.

44 Then he turned toward the woman and said to Simon, "Do you see this woman? I came into your house. You did not give me any water for my feet, but she wet my feet with her tears and wiped them with her hair. 45 You did not give me a kiss, but this woman, from the time I entered, has not stopped kissing my feet. 46 You did not put oil on my head, but she has poured perfume on my feet. 47 Therefore, I tell you, her many sins have been forgiven—as her great love has shown. But whoever has been forgiven little loves little."

48 Then Jesus said to her, "Your sins are forgiven."

49 The other guests began to say among themselves, "Who is this who even forgives sins?"

50 Jesus said to the woman, "Your faith has saved you; go in peace."

The Preparation:

COSTUME – The costume for this character should be a little flashy since this woman was very sinful for most of her life.

AGE – This character can be at any age.

BACKGROUND – This is a sinful woman. She appears to be very contrite and shows love to Jesus the only way she knows how.

DEMEANOR – Sorrowful, mournful. She sought out the only one who could help her - Jesus

The Story:

I was not someone you would invite into your home for dinner. I was not someone you would even speak to if you saw me on the streets. And I would be the last person in the world you would call a friend. And then again you would be the last person I would ever go to if I needed anything. Our worlds would have never collided. At least not before Jesus came into my life.

Everyone knew who I was. Small town. Everyone knew everyone. The good and the bad. I was the bad.

I had heard of Jesus; His miracles, His healings, His sermons. I was there, hidden in the crowd and I remembered the words that He spoke, "Blessed are you who are poor, . . . Blessed are you who hunger now, . . . Blessed are you who weep now, . . . Blessed are you when people hate you . . . "

I was mesmerized. He was saying those words to me, speaking straight to my heart. I was the one, in all that crowd, He was calling to Himself. Yet, I felt as if I was the most shameful, most undeserving person who ever walked the face of the earth. How could I have the "kingdom of God", how could I "be satisfied", or how could I . . . even "laugh"?

Those words seemed to haunt me and they kept ringing in my ears – not to condemn me, but to call to me to Jesus.

I cannot tell you how happy I was to hear that Jesus was coming to our town, to have dinner, but with a Pharisee. A Pharisee? This man pretended to be a religious do-gooder, but his sins were no better than mine and I should know it. If he could be in the presence of Jesus, so could I. I saw this as my chance to atone for my sins. I would offer a jar of perfume to Jesus. It was something of value I believed He could use. It was an expensive gift to me from someone I shall not mention.

I had no problem entering the house, I had been there before. But something happened as I approached Jesus. I became overwhelmed with guilt and grief, to the point of being uncontrollable. I began to weep profusely. Just being in the presence Him drew out every emotion within my being. I fell at His feet and my tears continued, wetting his feet. My hair flowed over His feet and I began to use my hair to wipe them and in my state of contriteness, I began to kiss His feet, and without thinking I poured the perfume over them.

As I continued, I heard the Pharisee speak to himself, "If this man were a prophet, he would know who is touching him and what kind of woman she is—that she is a sinner."

Jesus also heard this, but He did not try to stop me. Instead, he answered him, "Simon, I have something to tell you."

"Tell me, teacher," he said.

"Two people owed money to a certain moneylender. One owed him five hundred denarii, and the other fifty. Neither of them had the money to pay him back, so he forgave the debts of both. Now which of them will love him more?"

Simon replied, "I suppose the one who had the bigger debt forgiven."

"You have judged correctly," Jesus said.

Then he turned toward me and said to Simon, "Do you see this woman? I came into your house. You did not give me any water for my feet, but she wet my feet with her tears and wiped them with her hair. You did not give me a kiss, but this woman, from the time I entered, has not stopped kissing my feet. You did not put oil on my head, but she has poured perfume on my feet. Therefore, I tell you, her many sins have been forgiven—as her great love has shown. But whoever has been forgiven little loves little."

Then Jesus said to me, "Your sins are forgiven."

A lifetime of sinning had been wiped from my heart! Immediately, I began to rejoice and praise God. Words can not express the joy I was experiencing at that moment.

Soon after Jesus left our town and began to travel from place to place proclaiming the good news and healing others along the way. I too, began to travel with Him as did other women Jesus had healed. Mary Magdalene, Joanna and Susanna were such women and they were helping to support Jesus and His disciples out of their own means.

Not only did we help support them, but we also shared our faith with many other women in the town and villages we passed through. From that beginning, many women came to Christ and they too shared the faith with even more women, and that has continued throughout the ages.

THE WOMAN AT THE WELL

The Woman at the Well Costume

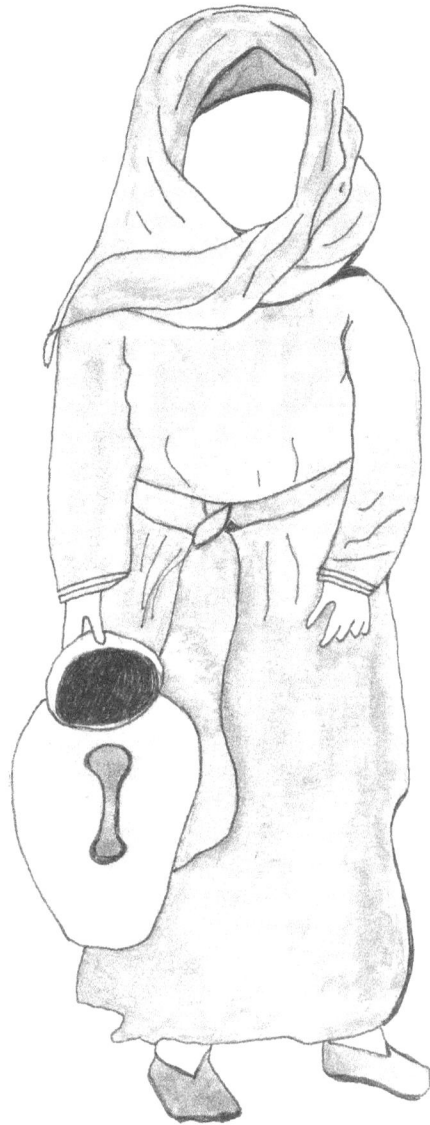

This costume is not fancy. No bright colors;. Some headpiece would be necessary. She is a sinful woman, yet she does not want to attract attention with her clothing. Water jug not necessary.

The Woman at the Well – John 4:3-30; 39-42

The Scripture:

3 So he left Judea and went back once more to Galilee.

4 Now he had to go through Samaria. 5 So he came to a town in Samaria called Sychar, near the plot of ground Jacob had given to his son Joseph. 6 Jacob's well was there, and Jesus, tired as he was from the journey, sat down by the well. It was about noon.

7 When a Samaritan woman came to draw water, Jesus said to her, "Will you give me a drink?" 8 (His disciples had gone into the town to buy food.)

9 The Samaritan woman said to him, "You are a Jew and I am a Samaritan woman. How can you ask me for a drink?" (For Jews do not associate with Samaritans.)

10 Jesus answered her, "If you knew the gift of God and who it is that asks you for a drink, you would have asked him and he would have given you living water."

11 "Sir," the woman said, "you have nothing to draw with and the well is deep. Where can you get this living water? 12 Are you greater than our father Jacob, who gave us the well and drank from it himself, as did also his sons and his livestock?"

13 Jesus answered, "Everyone who drinks this water will be thirsty again, 14 but whoever drinks the water I give them will never thirst. Indeed, the water I give them will become in them a spring of water welling up to eternal life."

15 The woman said to him, "Sir, give me this water so that I won't get thirsty and have to keep coming here to draw water."

16 He told her, "Go, call your husband and come back."

17 "I have no husband," she replied.

Jesus said to her, "You are right when you say you have no husband. 18 The fact is, you have had five husbands, and the man you now have is not your husband. What you have just said is quite true."

19 "Sir," the woman said, "I can see that you are a prophet. 20 Our ancestors worshiped on this mountain, but you Jews claim that the place where we must worship is in Jerusalem."

21 "Woman," Jesus replied, "believe me, a time is coming when you will worship the Father neither on this mountain nor in Jerusalem. 22 You Samaritans worship what you do not know; we worship what we do know, for salvation is from the Jews. 23 Yet a time is coming and has now come when the true worshipers will worship the Father in the Spirit and in truth, for they are the kind of worshipers the Father

seeks. ²⁴ God is spirit, and his worshipers must worship in the Spirit and in truth."

²⁵ The woman said, "I know that Messiah" (called Christ) "is coming. When he comes, he will explain everything to us."

²⁶ Then Jesus declared, "I, the one speaking to you—I am he.

²⁷ Just then his disciples returned and were surprised to find him talking with a woman. But no one asked, "What do you want?" or "Why are you talking with her?"

²⁸ Then, leaving her water jar, the woman went back to the town and said to the people, ²⁹ "Come, see a man who told me everything I ever did. Could this be the Messiah?" ³⁰ They came out of the town and made their way toward him.

³⁹ Many of the Samaritans from that town believed in him because of the woman's testimony, "He told me everything I ever did." ⁴⁰ So when the Samaritans came to him, they urged him to stay with them, and he stayed two days. ⁴¹ And because of his words many more became believers.

⁴² They said to the woman, "We no longer believe just because of what you said; now we have heard for ourselves, and we know that this man really is the Savior of the world."

The Preparation:

COSTUME – The costume for this character should be normal Bible-time clothes. A large pottery jar is nice but not required.

AGE – This character can be at any age as an adult.

BACKGROUND – This woman was living a life in sin and was looked down upon in her community.

DEMEANOR – She was ashamed for what she had done and would be very contrite.

The Story:

Do you have any idea what it's like to be an outcast in your own community; to be shunned and rejected by people you have known your whole life? At first, it's hard to accept and you start to blame yourself and then blame others. Later you blame your circumstances - you blame the times – you blame anyone and anything.

And then you come to the point where nothing matters anyway anymore. You finally accept you plight in life and you slip into a deep despair, a deep, bottomless hole that you know you will never get out of.

I avoided anyone and everyone. I gave up any kind of contact with the whole world.

Normal relationships with other humans did not exist. I felt doomed to a life of emptiness, meaninglessness and void.

I had the mistaken belief that men would satisfy my need for companionship. I thought they could provide me with hope and a promise of rising out of my anguish. I even failed at that.

I felt I had to dodge any contact with people. That's what happened that fateful day when I went to the well to gather water. It was going to be the moment in my life where everything, and I mean everything, would change.

It was the middle of the day – the hottest and dustiest part of the day – I would trudge to Jacob's well to find water. No one else would be there. Others had already gone in the early hours, when it was cooler, and the winds had not started blowing the dust across the village. At least I thought no one would be there.

As I approached the well, as I would do whenever I ventured away from my house, I kept my head down, never wanting to make eye contact with anyone else who may be out by chance.

Nearing the well, I was surprised to see someone sitting there, especially a man and a Jew at that. I knew not to make contact or even speak to Him for Jews were to have no association with a Samaritan.   But then I was startled when he spoke to me.

 "Will you give me a drink?"

I answered him, "You are a Jew and I am a Samaritan woman. How can you ask me for a drink?"

Then he answered, "If you knew the gift of God and who it is that asks you for a drink, you would have asked him, and he would have given you living water."

 "Sir," I said, "you have nothing to draw with and the well is deep. Where can you get this living water? Are you greater than our father Jacob, who gave us the well and drank from it himself, as did also his sons and his livestock?"

He paused and then answered, "Everyone who drinks this water will be thirsty again, but whoever drinks the water I give them will never thirst. Indeed, the water I give them will become in them a spring of water welling up to eternal life."

I said to him, "Sir, give me this water so that I won't get thirsty and have to keep coming here to draw water."

But then he said something to me that cut to my heart. He looked at me and said, "Go, call your husband and come back."

My first thought was to lie. How would he know the truth? I would just tell him I have no husband. He would never know the difference. I would lie.

Then quickly he came back to me, "You are right when you say you have no husband. The fact is, you have had five husbands, and the man you now have is not your husband. What you have just said is quite true."

I was stunned. How did he know this? He is hitting to close to home. I felt I needed o change the tone of our conversation.

"Sir," I said, "I can see that you are a prophet. Our ancestors worshiped on this mountain, but you Jews claim that the place where we must worship is in Jerusalem."

I was hoping my change of subject would deflect off me. But he would not leave it alone.

"Woman," he replied, "believe me, a time is coming when you will worship the Father neither on this mountain nor in Jerusalem. You Samaritans worship what you do not know; we worship what we do know, for salvation is from the Jews. Yet a time is coming and has now come when the true worshipers will worship the Father in the Spirit and in truth, for they are the kind of worshipers the Father seeks. God is spirit, and his worshipers must worship in the Spirit and in truth."

I said, "I know that Messiah, the one called Christ, is coming. When he comes, he will explain everything to us."

Then he declared, "I, the one speaking to you—I am he".

Just then more men came to the place of the well and seemed surprised to find him talking with me. Yet no one asked, "What do you want?" or "Why are you talking with her?"

At that moment I knew I was in the presence of the Christ we all were expecting. For the first time in a long time, I knew I needed go back to town and share with the other villagers about this man. It didn't matter what I felt others thought of me. This was the good news.

Then, I left my water jar, and went back to the town to tell the people,

I banged on doors, I shouted through windows, I interrupted those selling and buying in the marketplace, "Come, see a man who told me everything I ever did." I was telling everyone, "Could this be the Messiah?"

They came out of the town and made their way toward him.

Many of the Samaritans from that town believed in him because of my testimony when I told them all, "He told me everything I ever did."

So, when the Samaritans came to him, they urged him to stay with them, and he stayed two days. And because of his words many more became believers.

Many in the village said to me, "We no longer believe just because of what you said; now we have heard for ourselves, and we know that this man really is the Savior of the world."

Later I learned the man's name was Jesus. The interesting thing is he never condemned me or passed judgement on me, but he did make me realized He was the only one who could meet my needs. Before Jesus, I had been condemned and ridiculed most of my life. People had been very cruel to me. Yet Jesus showed me love and compassion. He looked beyond my sins and saw the value of one individual. A man who spoke to thousands, took the time to speak to me - just me.

Two thoughts I leave with you. First, God see great value in each human heart. We need to follow his example and believe in the worth of every person. And second, show the love of Jesus to everyone. My being was a wreck. I was in the depths of a sinful life, yet Jesus did not condemn me nor denounce me. Always we must love the unlovable. Jesus showed that to me. Let's show that to others.

COMING SOON!
Ordinary People – Extraordinary God – Volume 3

This collection of monologues will include:

- A Dead Girl Rises

- Man's Son with a Demonic Spirit

- The Woman with the Issue of Blood

- Jesus Heals a Blind Man

- Jesus Drives Out an Unclean Spirit

- Jesus Speaks to the Little Children

- Jesus Heals the Deaf Man

- Woman's Daughter with the Impure Spirit

- Jesus Raises a Widow's Son

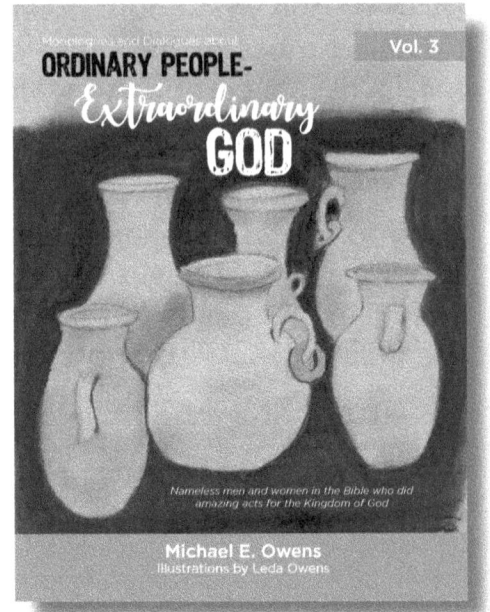

Watch for the release date for this book and others written by Michael E. Owens on the following social media and websites:

- Website - www.booksbyMEO.com

- Book Orders - www.scribblersweb.com

- Facebook - @booksbymeo

- Twitter - @mikeandfriends2

- Facebook - @booksbyMEO

- Instagram – bookbyMEO

- Podcast - "The Mike and Friends 2 Show"

- Also check out "Santa Mike and Leda Claus" on Facebook

Patterns for Bible Costumes

If you are looking for patterns to sew Bible costumes, check out the following patterns which may be available at your local fabric shop or online:

McCall's #2339

McCall's #2060

Simplicity #4795

Other Titles Available from Michael E. Owens
Available from Scribblersweb.com and Amazon

The I Hate Vegetables Book of Poetry for Kids

The "I Hate Vegetables Book of Poetry for Kids" is a fun, whimsical and irreverent look at the veggies kids hate to eat the most. It's a book to be enjoyed by those who hate vegetables as well as those who love them! Please – read and be entertained! (and eat your veggies!)

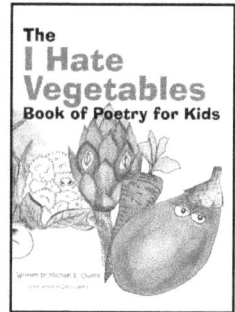

Does the River Ever End?

It's the 1840s along the Mississippi River and Mike Fink must live in the shadow of his infamous father, with no one giving him a fair shake. Mike and a slave, Cletus, believing they will be charged for two murders on the riverboat, escape capture through the backwoods of Illinois, down the Ohio and Mississippi Rivers, heading as far away from Cairo as they can. Being chased by the law and outlaws too, will Mike and Cletus finally make it to Memphis and freedom?

Summer of Heroes

In the 1870's, Billy was looking forward to a lazy summer in West Texas, waiting for his dad to return home to take their cattle to market. When he doesn't return, the task of trail boss lands in his lap. On his travels with the herd, he gains an unexpected trail hand and runs into a band of rustlers, the man the Chisholm trail is named after, Bass Reeves, the first black Texas Ranger, and a famous Indian chief. On his return home, he has another unexpected visitor and goes after his dream – a wild stallion in the hills. Billy never considered himself a hero, but others had a different idea.

Coming Soon!

Eggs! Eggs! Eggs!

Peter Rabbit is running short of painted Easter Eggs for all the good boys and girls. The forest animals, who paint the eggs, are beginning to become overwhelmed. Their new invention seems to be the answer until it is stolen by the Evil Woodsman. But thanks to the daffy Wood Fairy, everything turns out great! A wonderful musical for younger grades and special needs.

Santa Checks His List Around the World

Take a ride with Santa as he visits the children of the world, one country at a time. Egypt, Canada, Greece, Scandinavia, China, Ireland, Mexico and other countries too!

www.ingramcontent.com/pod-product-compliance
Lightning Source LLC
Chambersburg PA
CBHW080527110426
42742CB00017B/3263